P9-DOG-452

Who Stole My Cheese?!!

A Parody

Praise for Ilene Hochberg's Books

STORIES WITH INSIGHTS INTO THE PEOPLE AND
PET BOND. WITH ANIMALS YOU ALWAYS KNOW
WHO YOUR FRIENDS ARE.

DOGUE

*"We doubt if you'll ever see a funnier parody...*Dogue *is without a doubt a Best of Show in the parody class."* —Malcolm Forbes
FORBES MAGAZINE

*"*Dogue *is so successful that most of the publishing world has been left with its tail between its legs...and sales have gone through the woof."*
—PEOPLE MAGAZINE

"If anyone is an authority on the changing role of dogs and cats in American society, it ought to be Hochberg." —NEWSWEEK MAGAZINE

"I love your book and gave away 350 of them at a benefit for the Humane Society of New York." —Bill Blass, designer

"Woof woof, I just loved your gorgeous Dogue *magazine and brilliantly sexy-wexy photography."* —Helmut Newton, photographer

"Fashion has gone to the dogs, literally and brilliantly, in a clever takeoff of Vogue*...called* Dogue. Vogue *Editor in Chief Grace Mirabella says that she hasn't seen it yet but got a phone call from Bill Blass, who loved it."*
—Nina Hyde, fashion editor
THE WASHINGTON POST

*"With breezy, snobbish prose and stunning use of color...*Dogue *successfully plays on the essence of* Vogue*...a meticulous, hilarious send-up...Publishers Weekly Choice: The Year's Best Books."* —PUBLISHERS WEEKLY

"If Diana Vreeland owned a pooch, he would...have a lifetime subscription to Dogue, *the hilarious, doggie-bone-in-cheek parody of 'the world's most famous fashion magazine.'"* —NEW YORK MAGAZINE

CATMOPOLITAN

"Catmopolitan *(this year's* Dogue*)* is another big hit....Our biggest book for the whole Christmas season." —PUBLISHERS WEEKLY

"This purr-ody cat-egorically is the latest thing for feline fanciers...What does Helen Gurley Brown think of such shenanigans? She loves it." —Liz Smith, syndicated columnist

"Whoever said it's a dog eat dog world has obviously never met Hochberg." —THE ROBB REPORT

"Dogue...the wickedly funny and extremely successful lampoon of Vogue...Catmopolitan, an often searing exposé of life in the feline fast lane." —ADVERTISING AGE

"Think your feline's divine? ...Check out Catmopolitan, a magazine spoof from the creator of Dogue. —USA TODAY

VANITY FUR

"Your Vanity Fur is the cat's meow! We're all purring from your brilliant spoof." —Tina Brown, editor in chief VANITY FAIR MAGAZINE

"Another brilliant book...Well done, sophisticated, clever, and really classy." —UNITED MEDIA

Who Stole My Cheese?!!

should be used by men, women, and rats in many corporations, governmental agencies, the military, small businesses, hospitals, churches, schools, and penitentiaries, including:

Adealphia Corporation • ALL Time Waster • Artful Andersen • Bristol-Lyers-Criibb • NO Energy • Citicorrupt • Darken Energy • Crusties • Dizzy • Duped Energy • Lynegy • Im Passe • Encon • GWhiz • Global Doublecrossing • Helliburton • Homeinvasion.com • Cloneim • Not OKmart • Lucre Technologies • Martha Stewed Living Omnipotent • Murky • Merryll Lynched • Myrant • Nocorp, LLP • Pergatory Systems • Quest Miscommunications International • Unreliant Energy • Soldout Smith Smarmy • Sothebid • Stanley Doesn't Work • Lieco • Winsome Losesome Communications • WorldCon

WHO STOLE MY CHEESE?!!

"*Every once in a while a book comes along that opens the door to a prison. This book had that effect on me.*"   —*Sam Weasel, former CEO*
CLONEIM

"*As soon as I finished reading this, I ordered copies to help us deal with the unexpected changes we'll face—from being in charge of a corporate dynasty to being incarcerated.*"   —*John Rigs, former CEO*
ADEALPHIA

"*I can picture myself reading this wonderful story to my children and grand-children in the prison's visitors' room, and their understanding the lessons.*"
     —*Alfred Tubman, former CEO*
SOTHEBID

"*The book's enticing images and simple language give us a foolproof way of harnessing greed.*"   —*Dennis Kozlousy, former CEO*
LIECO

"*Our unique insights and skill with a pen make this the rare book that can be read and understood quickly by everyone who wants to get rich without regard for the consequences.*"   —*Ken Lie, former CEO*
ENCON

"*This book is a simple, understandable road map for us to use to navigate toward wealth despite our present incarceration.*"
     —*Bernie Embers, former CEO*
WORLDCON

"*I'd never share my trade secrets with anyone if I wasn't going to make a lot of money from doing so. I'm still better than you are at doing* everything!*"*
     —*Martha Stewed, CEO*
MARTHA STEWED LIVING OMNIPOTENT

"*Now I know why we increased the penalties for white collar crime!*"
     —*Dick Cheesey, Vice President of the United States*
Former CEO, HELLIBURTON

Books by Ilene Hochberg

DOGUE
CATMOPOLITAN
VANITY FUR
FORBABES
GOOD MOUSEKEEPING

Who Stole My Cheese?!!

An A-Mazing Way To Make More Money
From The Poor Suckers That You Cheated
In Your Work And In Your Life

A Parody by

Ilene Hochberg

UNION SQUARE PRESS
New York

Dedicated to my husband, Irwin Hochberg,
who taught me everything I know about business and life.
And to my friend Albert Salama, who actually reads these books!

With love and appreciation to my two families.
Family by birth: Trudy Berhang, Dr. Bernard Rosenthal, Holly and
Howard Bernstein, Joelle and Bradley Silverman, Malvina and Joseph Farkas

Family by choice: Irwin Hochberg, Selig Zises, Jay and Nancy Zises,
Lynn and Doug Krugman, Carl D'Aquino, Jose Valdes-Fauli, Shed Boren,
Anya and Albert Salama, Stephanie Freed, Jeanne Mathews, Jack Hruska, Ralph Lutrin,
Allan Lewis, Thierry Soursac, Eric and Myra Outwater, Carol Hochberg, Gail and
Steven Hochberg, Lindy and Seth Hochberg, Hayleigh, Alex, Rachel, and
Daniel Hochberg, Tori Pines Hochberg, Barguzin 'Bargie' Hochberg, Nubie Hochberg,
Michael Fragnito, Alan Kahn, Meredith Peters, Peter Miller, Paul Kezmarsky, Brad Feuer

A Union Square Press Book
An Imprint of the Barnes & Noble Publishing Group
Copyright 2002 © by Ilene Hochberg

Library of Congress Cataloging-in-Publication Data available upon request

Who Stole My Cheese?!! An A-Mazing Way To Make More Money
From the Poor Suckers That You Cheated In Your Work and In Your Life

ISBN 1-58663-931-5

Printed and bound in the United States of America

3 5 7 9 10 8 6 4 2

First Edition

The best laid schemes
o' weasels and rats
often go astray.

Bobby Burns
1759–1796

———

If they smell a ratt, they grisely chide
And chatt.

John Skelton, Image of Hypocracy
1550

———

You dirty rat.

James Cagney, Blonde Crazy
1931

Who Stole My Cheese?!!

CONTENTS

Parts of All of Us 12

The Story Behind the Scandal
By Kenneth Lie, former CEO 13

A Gathering: Allenwood 23

The Story of Who Stole My Cheese?!! 33
Six Characters
Stealing Cheese
Where's My Cheese?
The Rats: Snivel & Scurvy
The Loyal Employees: Hid & Hah
The Boss and His Lackey, The Accountant Andersen
Paralyzed With Fear
Enjoy the Process
The Work Will Make You Free
The Shredded Evidence
Stealing New Cheese
Enjoying Control!

A Dissection: Recreational Break 81

Share It With Everyone .91
About the Author 92

PARTS OF ALL OF US

The Simple and The Corrupt

The six imaginary characters depicted in this story—
the rats: "Snivel" and "Scurvy,"
the loyal employees: "Hid" and "Hah," and
The Boss and his lackey, The Accountant Andersen—
are intended to represent the simple and the corrupt
parts of ourselves without regard for the consequences.

Sometimes we may act like
Snivel
Who whines about change, or
Scurvy
Who skulks about changing secretly, or
Hid
Who craves routine as he fears that anything else will
lead to something worse than poverty, or
Hah
Who learns to adapt by rejecting all conscience, and
laughs at the consequences as he moves onto
something better, or
The Boss and his lackey, The Accountant Andersen
Who call all the shots and shred all the evidence in
their never ending quest for ultimate control and
fantastic compensation despite deplorable performance.

Whatever parts we choose to use, we all share
something in common: a sense of entitlement,
unbridled greed, and a total lack of conscience.

And that is our cheesy formula for success.

The Story Behind The Scandal
by Kenneth Lie, former CEO, Encon

I am thrilled to be telling you "the story behind the scandal" of *Who Stole My Cheese?!!* because it means that the book has been written, and we can now sit back and wait for the money to roll in.

This is something I've wanted to see happen since I first heard my colleagues commiserating about how to get rich by screwing their corporations and stockholders. I want to thank Bernie Embers, John Rigs, Gary Whining, Dennis Kozlousy, Alfred Tubman, Jack Grubby, Sam Weasel, but especially Jeff Skimming, Andy Fastbuck, Joe Buriedinero, Michael Kopout, my wife Linda Lie, and Martha Stewed for inspiring this book, and contributing to its successful completion.

I remember thinking about how valuable this advice was and that people would pay good money to read it. Even those people who had lost money through the stock manipulations and bad business decisions that benefited only my colleagues. *Especially* those people. Because it was the employees and investors in my colleagues' corporations (okay, mine too) who lost their jobs and life savings. They have to come up with a new strategy to recoup their losses, so they are the perfect market for this book.

Who Stole My Cheese?!! is a story about the changes that take place in the lives of the four little characters trapped in a maze, and of the two large characters who stand over the maze looking in. They are all looking for "Cheese," which is a metaphor for what we want in life—a job, romance, fast car, big house, time for golf and travel, but especially great wealth and riches so we can *buy* all the other stuff I have mentioned. In other words: Cheese = $.

Everyone has his own formula for happiness, but whatever it is that you value, you can buy it with lots of money. And even if you can't (which isn't often), you can buy other great stuff that will take your mind off what you *can't* have. So, money is our ultimate goal.

My colleagues have figured this out, and they have devised a unique way of accumulating wealth without a lot of effort. My colleagues use their employees and investors to "find their cheese."

That's right, we use *you* to get our money. And the best part is that we have manipulated you into believing that you are working for your own benefit and advancement, when in fact, you are working only to make us richer than you could ever imagine.

Do you live in a mansion, or have homes all over the world? Do you fly from place to place on private jets? Do you wear designer clothes, collect art and antiques, and dine in the finest restaurants? Do you vacation in luxurious hotels, or belong to the best country clubs?

We do. And we're taking your money, from your hard work, to pay for it all. And that's the cheesy truth....

I tell the "Cheese" story that you are about to read in my community service required talks. It was part of my sentence.

You see, the government caught onto our gambit, and the politicians got jealous that we were stealing even more money than they were. When the public began to examine special interest groups and soft money, the politicians got scared and gave us up to save their own reputations.

The government began to investigate the way we did business and before we knew it, we became public enemy number one. They even changed the penalties for white-collar crimes from a maximum of five years in a country club prison to twenty years of hard time.

So we were forced to put our heads together to devise a new way to make money—and from behind bars, no less.

That explains this book. We have written about how we manipulated the market and our employees to accumulate riches beyond measure.

It's easy for us to pass along these secrets, mainly because they have changed the rules and our old methods won't work anymore.

We're giving you ice in winter, useless information, and you're paying us yet again for this lesson in greed.

We're buying time, keeping busy, and making money from prison to pay our high-priced lawyers for our appeals. And once again, you're paying the price for our corporate chicanery.

Believe it or not, this little story has been credited with saving our careers and lives.

One of the many real life examples comes from my own experience. I ran a huge corporation, which I treated like my personal piggy bank. I had enlisted the aid of my trusty accomplices, I mean colleagues, at Encon: Jeff Skimming, Andy Fastbuck, and my accountant Joe Buriedinero from Artful Andersen. We cleverly devised a plan to pump up the value of our stock and hide all our losses through an intricate means, which involved the creation of a series of bogus partnerships, divisions, and "outside" investments. Don't ask me how they did it. I don't know anything about it. I was only running the company. I was too busy being in charge to pay attention to those small details.

Our CEO Fastbuck took care of getting it done with the help of his associate, Michael Kopout. When the bottom fell out of our creative accounting practices, our whole corporation began to unravel.

I thought I was home free. Linda and I are close personal friends of George and Laura, and I had made sure that Encon was the largest corporate contributor to Clinton's presidential campaign, just to cover all the bases.

But the government wouldn't be happy until they made this little issue into a federal case. I was up to my end in examiners. They put the heat to Fastbuck's little assistant. He began to spill his guts in a desperate attempt to save his own hide. Before long they were all over Andy, and right after that they were onto me.

I had a penthouse in Houston and vacation homes in Aspen, with antiques and art in each one. We were happy just to live our lives on a smaller scale, close to home. But when the story began to explode in the headlines, they had to find a scapegoat. Linda and I were the easiest marks. Suddenly we were under suspicion. I had to find a way to raise money for my defense and damage control. I was forced to change direction.

I had to sell a couple of my homes in Aspen, and Linda had to go to work in a shop to sell "jus stuff." She even went on television, crying, to admit to the world that we were broke. (Thank goodness for waterproof mascara, she said, or she would have ended up looking like Tammy Fay Baker.)

We were down to our last 70 million, and we were forced to live in our penthouse. I don't know how you would weather that reversal in fortune, but we tightened the belt and moved forward. When life gave us lemons, we made lemonade.

That explains this book.

The book is divided into three sections. The first, *A Gathering,* is a group of us talking about our predicament over lunch in the prison cafeteria, where we devise the plan for this book.

The second section is *The Story Of Who Stole My Cheese?!!,* which is the heart of the book. This short, insipid tale uses overly simplistic language and imagery to tell our complex story to even the most naïve or uneducated reader. We want to sell a lot of books, so we have told our story in terms that are readily understood by even the lowest common denominator.

In the third section, *A Dissection,* we examine what the story, and this book, have meant to us. How it will benefit us in our new lives.

Some readers prefer to stop at the end of *The Story.* They can't bear to read another word of this drivel. Some readers can't even get that far.

In any case, we don't care how much of the story you read, or if you are able to incorporate any of its lessons into your life. We only care that you buy a copy, and recommend it to your friends. We want to sell a lot of books.

I hope you enjoy this little book. Remember: find your own "Cheese" while you help us find ours.

Ken Lie
Allenwood, Pennsylvania

This story is a fable,
a fairy tale,
a nightmare…
in other words,
a work of *complete* fiction.
All characters are made up
(real people couldn't be like this)
and any resemblance to anyone,
living or dead,
is really, really coincidental.

A Gathering
Allenwood

One murky Monday in Pennsylvania, several former business colleagues, who had served on the same boards of corporations, gathered for lunch in the prison cafeteria. They wanted to hear more about what had led each of them to this unfortunate place. After some sarcastic banter and a sad meal of bland stew and cold coffee, they settled into yet another conversation about what had brought them all here.

Martha Stewed, who had moved seamlessly from cheerleader and homecoming queen to Queen of All Media said, "My life has turned out differently than I planned. I thought I had everything under control. But they changed the rules."

"They certainly have," John Rigs replied. He had gone into his family business, and had joined with his sons, Timothy and Michael, to build Adealphia into a cable and communications empire. They had even taken company earnings to build a personal golf course, which was permissible under the old rules of the game. But not now. He asked, "Have you noticed that just when things are going well for us, the government changes the rules? I thought *we* were in charge. But I'm afraid we're not any more."

Ken Lie said, "I guess we resist change because we thought we made all the rules."

Each of them was struggling to cope with the unexpected changes that had happened to them in recent years. And all had to admit that they did not see an end to their unfortunate predicament.

"Ken, you were the CEO of one of the largest and most profitable companies in the country. You had a salary and benefits beyond compare. And now we're all here. What went wrong?" Dennis Kozlousy asked. "I thought that way of life would never end. I miss my office at Lieco, my homes and my jets and my fabulous art collection. And I had just gotten onto the board at the Whitney."

"I don't know what went wrong," answered Ken. "I was just doing my job, business as usual, pumping up the stock price, issuing myself and my colleagues lots of options, keeping up the motivation. I didn't do anything that each of you hasn't done a hundred times before. What happened? How did we end up in here?"

"They changed the rules," said Jeff Skimming. "They got jealous of who we were and all we had, so they had to find a way to take it all away from us. We didn't do anything wrong."

"That's not the worst part," said Bernie Embers of WorldCon. "We have to accept that they changed the rules. That we're all in here for the long haul. But we have to figure out a way to stay sane and productive."

"What do you suggest?" asked Joe Buriedinero. "What should we do while we're here? At Artful Andersen I was good at manipulating money."

"Well, the most important thing is to *make* money. That's what we do. Just because they have us locked up like animals doesn't mean that we have to behave like we're restrained," Bernie answered.

"Do you have any ideas?" asked Sam Weasel, who was still disoriented from the loss of Cloneim.

"Sure. I have a million of them," said Martha. "That's what they pay me for."

"But we're in jail. They may call it a 'country club jail' or 'Club Fed,' but we're still locked up," said Andy Fastbuck.

"Yes. But that's what makes it fun. It's a challenge to be successful from 'the inside.' We've made it before. We can do it again," said Bernie.

"I think you've been teaching too much Sunday school. You sound like a preacher, or a motivational speaker. Just how can we make it from in here?" asked Alfred Tubman, the former CEO of Sothebid. "I don't see any way to fix prices if we don't have a product or service."

"Motivational speaking isn't a bad idea," replied Gary Whining, who had run Global Doublecrossings. "Maybe they can pay us to speak to our fellow inmates about how to use our time in the corrections system for personal improvement. Character enhancement. Vocational training. Perhaps we can teach them how to buy and trade stock online?"

"But where is the income stream? I don't see where you would make any money. The Department of Corrections would keep any proceeds above the 11 cents an hour that they pay us inside for our work. At that pay scale, we could work non-stop throughout our sentences and make less than we used to spend for a bottle of good wine at lunch. The economics just don't add up," said Joe.

"He's right. We'll have to do better than that. Perhaps if we organized the prison and went out on a strike for better wages. I've seen it done," said Michael Kopout.

"You and your bright ideas," stormed Andy. "If it weren't for you, I'd never be in here. And that goes for Jeff and Ken, too. We're all in here because of your weak liberal attitudes. Since when do you equate us with the rank and file workers? It's thoughts like that which put us here in the first place. The minute they took away your 12 and a half million dollars, you began to think like a common Joe. With an attitude like that, you didn't deserve your money."

Martha smiled smugly, then offered her suggestion. "Why don't we write a book? I know something about publishing, and a book can be very lucrative. We won't need any special skills or materials. We all have interesting stories to tell. Let's collect our thoughts and package them for sale."

"That's not a bad idea," said Jack Grubby of Soldout Smith Smarmy. "It might be a good way to make the time pass while we're in here, and we can see a good profit upon our release."

"You don't understand. I'm not talking about a long-term effort. I'm not looking at wasting months, or years, on self-indulgent blather. I'm talking about doing a book. Right now. While our story is hot and timely. And publishing it to make money," she said impatiently.

"You mean an 'instant' book? I've read about those," said Dennis.

"Exactly. We get it done and out there. Then we gauge its success to determine additional marketing opportunities. The magazine...the miniseries...the sitcom...the licensed goods.... We can have a field day if the subject is right," Martha said with a smile.

"She's right. We can make a lot of money in the ancillary markets," said Dennis. "Let's put our heads together to plan this correctly. We all have something we can contribute. It's a good way to make some money for when we get out of here. I only have a couple of hundred to fall back on. And I did enjoy living well."

They all smiled wistfully when they remembered how they had lived on the outside. And they took some small solace in the fact that they were all in here together. Perhaps this plan could work.

"What should we write about? What would be the most compelling topic, something that people would pay good money to read?" asked Sam.

"An exposé about our life in here might be good. Those 'women behind bars' things always seem to do well. How about 'CEOs Behind Bars?'" asked Michael.

"I think it's a little too tawdry. Even though we're in prison, we have to maintain a sense of dignity," said Ken.

"You're right," Bernie replied. "Let's look and see if we can take the high road to success. Just like last time."

They sat together silently, their coffee growing icy in their metal mugs.

"We're all leaders in business," Bernie said. "Let's use that premise as a point of departure. What can we tell people that they would pay to learn? Perhaps a book which outlines our business successes would be a good idea."

"That's a good start," said Andy. "But I'm not sure that they would allow us to keep our money. They'd see it as a way of making money from our purported 'crimes.' I think we should consult our attorneys to find a loophole so that we could keep the proceeds from this or any other project which might flow from this concept."

"He's right," said Ken. "I've spent a good amount of time, and money, working with lawyers recently, as I'm certain you have all done as well. There must be a way to keep the money, or earmark it for some approved purpose."

"I'll bet they would let us make money to pay for our legal expenses. You can be sure that our clever, and high priced, legal advisers could find a way to execute that plan. It would kill two birds with one stone," said John.

"You're right. We can say that we need the money for our defense. Let's pool our talents to 'raise money for our legal expenses.' Those lawyers have us trapped in this maze until we can pay them to mount our new appeal. We'll put them to work to earn their own fees. It's the best way to go. After all, we can't touch our offshore accounts or they'd really penalize us by taking back all our money!" said Ken.

"That's right," said Bernie. "I've got a great idea. Let's write a book that shows the little people how we made our fortunes. How we put them, and others, to work for us. How we used them to make ourselves rich. They'd pay good money for those secrets. And besides, now that the rules have been changed, we can't lose anything by telling them how we did it. Let's rip them off for a little more while we devise a new method to get rich. This is just a new way to take their money."

"Bernie, you're amazing," Martha said. "Your idea is brilliant. It's a way to turn our situation around. From losing everything—our freedom, reputation, and, worst of all, our money—to gaining something: more money!"

"You're right. It's a great idea. We can write a book, a little book, of rules for success. It won't take us long. We know what to do," said Gary.

"Just like Martha said. Quick. Instant. Short and sweet. In and out," said Jack.

"A new book of rules for success in our time," Bernie said with a smile. "Our trade 'secrets.' Everyone would buy it. We can even give it a cheesy feel-good ending so the readers will think that they've learned something useful and will recommend it to their friends. I'm sure that the parole board will look favorably upon us for our sense of 'restitution' and 'community service,' and will shave a few years off our sentences."

"That's perfect! You know," Martha said in a huff, "at first I was annoyed with the obvious simplicity of your plan, but then I was really annoyed with myself for not doing it first and publishing it on my own before I ended up in here! But being in here has changed me. Softened me. Taught me to share, a little. We'll put our differences aside and get the story down on paper. Then we'll sell it to the suckers while we devise our next plan on how to rip them off again!"

The Story of Who Stole My Cheese?!!

ONCE upon a time, in a land far away (or maybe not so far away, you be the judge) lived four little characters, trapped in a maze, looking for cheese to nourish them and make them happy. That was their first mistake.

Two were rats named "Snivel" and "Scurvy," and two were loyal employees—individuals who were as small as rats but looked and acted a lot like the members of middle management do today. Their names were "Hid" and "Hah."

They appeared small and almost insignificant. But if you watched them, you would immediately recognize their importance in the greater scheme of things. They did the work. They made it happen.

Every day, the rats and the loyal employees ran through the maze looking for "cheese."

The rats, Snivel and Scurvy, used their primitive rodent brains and animal instincts to search for cheese to eat. Basic sustenance was their simple goal.

The two loyal employees, Hid and Hah, used their more complex people brains, encumbered by useless beliefs and emotions, to search for a very different cheese, the metaphorical kind. Years of reading self-help and motivational literature had deluded them into thinking that they had control over their destinies. How wrong they were.

As different as the rats and loyal employees were, they shared something in common: indentured servitude to The Boss. So, every day they put on tiny business suits and running shoes, left their little homes, and rushed into the maze looking for cheese.

The maze was a labyrinth of corridors and chambers, with identical cubicles and workstations. It was an easy place for workers to get lost.

However, for those who found a way out of the monotonous and mind-numbing routine, (which wasn't very often) the maze held out the hope of a way to a better life. Or so it seemed.

The rats, Snivel and Scurvy, used the simple sniff and scurry method of finding cheese. Snivel would sniff along the maze corridors, grumbling to himself in an attempt to scare away anyone who might be following. Scurvy would run down other dark pathways, his eyes darting wildly and his ragged claws scratching ominously on the ground in his own frightening and secretive quest for cheese. They admired The Boss and felt a deep kinship to him on a primal level. Somewhere, far back in time, they were once related.

Like the rats, the two loyal employees, Hid and Hah, also searched for cheese. They were encumbered by the baggage of too many motivational seminars and corporate pep talks to think clearly. Their small minds were filled with conflicting philosophies on how to achieve success, and they were frustrated by their confusion. Yet, like loyal employees everywhere, they wanted to create a positive impression upon The Boss and be eligible for promotion. So they said all the right things, and kept their dissatisfaction to themselves.

Nevertheless, Snivel, Scurvy, Hid, and Hah all discovered, in their own way, what they were seeking. At the end of every day, each had achieved a small measure of success. They found lots of cheese for The Boss, and managed to taste a little of it themselves. They deposited all the cheese at the corporate cheese station for processing. That was the accepted procedure. And the company prospered.

Every morning, the rats and the loyal employees would dress in appropriate business attire and accumulate cheese. At the end of the day, they would deposit the cheese for processing. Before long, this became their standard routine.

Snivel and Scurvy, being rats, would run through the maze every day. They never varied their routine. They were dumb animals.

At the beginning, Hid and Hah also ran through the maze, eager to make a good impression upon The Boss. They were collecting good reviews and were biding their time until the next evaluation.

But after a while, without any positive feedback from management, the loyal employees began to slack off.

Hid and Hah woke a little later every day, dressed more slowly, and walked, rather than ran, through the maze. After all, the cheese would be there when they arrived at their cubicles.

Hid and Hah now dressed in casual khakis all week long, and became as comfortable as cogs in the system. They found lots of cheese for The Boss, and managed to eat a little of it every day themselves.

It wasn't long before Hid and Hah began to feel just the slightest bit of apathy toward their work. They had faith in the company, and felt secure in their employment. They even began to invest in the Corporate Cheese Plan, hoping to become fully vested upon retirement. In other words, they had been lulled into a false sense of security.

They bought small homes closer to the maze, and built a social life filled with company picnics and bowling leagues.

To feel cozier in their cubicles, Hid and Hah decorated their desks with cute coffee mugs and bobbing head rats. They hung up prints of dreamy sunsets and colorful rainbows depicted in soft focus photography. They even hung their own motivational posters, which featured images of cheese over clever captions that revealed The Boss's rules for success. One read:

Stealing Cheese Makes Me Happy.

They never really read the caption. They should have seen the writing on the wall, but they were lulled into compliance by the monotony of their daily routine.

Sometimes Hid and Hah would take their wives by their cubicles to admire their piles of cheese and their pretty mugs and posters.

"We're invaluable to the system. We're building toward a greater success. Soon we'll retire to our mortgage-free little homes and eat pension cheese for the remainder of our retirement days," they said to their wives.

Every evening the loyal employees would return home, their thoughts filled with visions of a secure future, and every day they would head to the office in an effort to find cheese to fulfill that dream.

This went on for quite a while. Soon Hid and Hah's confidence grew into a sense of entitlement. They wanted more of the cheese they had found for themselves.

But The Boss, observing their actions from above the maze, began to notice their dissatisfaction even before they recognized it for themselves.

The Boss had to keep them in line. The cheese was all his. He needed loyal employees to deliver that cheese. He had to teach them a lesson. He would change the rules.

The Boss sat down with The Accountant Andersen to devise a plan for The Boss to divert more cheese to his own benefit. They would back into the numbers and cook the books. The Boss would show record annual profits and be eligible for a year-end bonus. The stock in the company would go up and The Boss would exercise all the stock options he had given to himself. Then he would take a big raise in annual compensation, and in that way would steal all of the cheese.

The Boss had The Accountant Andersen work out the details. The Accountant would create a false set of books to support The Boss's new financial demands, and he would shred all the old books to destroy the evidence.

The Accountant Andersen would paint a rosy picture of the company's future in The Annual Report. It would reassure the loyal employees that they were building toward a secure future, and would also serve to attract fresh investment dollars from potential new stockholders.

The Accountant Andersen even built in a bit of additional revenue for himself in the form of a lucrative consulting contract with the corporation. One hand washes the other....

One morning, the rats, Snivel and Scurvy, arrived at their cubicles and found that the cheese was gone. They weren't surprised. Generations of evolution had prepared them to smell another rat.

The rats, utilizing their natural instincts, set off to sniff out more cheese.

The loyal employees, Hid and Hah, arrived at their workstations an hour later, prepared to languish in their cheese-filled environment. But all of their cheese was gone!

Hid cried out in anguish, "Where's my cheese?"

Hah, who was the angrier and more aggressive employee, cut to the chase. "Who *stole* my cheese?!!" he exclaimed loudly, and his voice could be heard throughout the office complex.

Hid grew numb with fear. Where had all the cheese gone? He had mortgage payments. Where would he find more cheese?

Hah grew vindictive. He began to plot about how he would locate the cheese and steal it back.

Hid began to cry. How would he tell his wife? How could he have been this trusting, this stupid?

Hah couldn't focus upon Hid's cries of anguish. He had his own problems. Hah had to find that cheese. And he had to do it before Hid suspected what was going on. There may not be enough left for both of them. Hah had to find that cheese first.

The loyal employees' behavior was not particularly attractive or ethical, but it was understandable. After all, they had been screwed by The Boss and the corporation. They were entitled to find some way of obtaining compensation for all their hard work.

Finding the cheese hadn't been easy. They had worked long hours and had earned positive personnel reviews. They had hit all their targets and achieved all their incremental goals.

Cheese wasn't just something to feed their bellies and pay their bills. Cheese was intricately tied into their identities and self-worth.

For some, cheese was the way to good health and well being.

For others, cheese was a currency that bought credibility in the social scheme.

To Hid, cheese provided the means for a good house and economic security.

To Hah, cheese was the key to prestige. He was on his way to becoming "a big cheese," as it were, in the corporation. He couldn't lose the scent of it now.

Because cheese was important to the loyal employees, for different reasons, Hid and Hah spent a long time deciding what to do next. They kept looking at their empty cubicles in disbelief.

While the rats, Snivel and Scurvy, had scurried along into the maze to look for more cheese, Hid and Hah remained paralyzed, unable to move on.

They threw temper tantrums, and beat upon their desks. They smashed their mugs in frustration, and tore the heads off the bobble dolls. How could this happen? How could they recoup their position? Who stole their cheese? And could they steal it back?

The loyal employees couldn't believe their misfortune. How did this happen, after years of devotion to the company and loyalty to The Boss? Just when they were on the cusp of a promotion, they lost their footing in the system.

Hid and Hah went home depressed and dejected. But before they left, Hah took a shard from his broken mug and scratched the following motto from The Boss into the cubicle wall:

The More Important You Are,
The More Cheese
You Want To Hold Onto.

The next day, Hid and Hah got to the office a little earlier than usual, half expecting to see all their cheese. Maybe it had been a bad dream.

But their cubicles were empty. Nothing had changed overnight. Hid and Hah stood frozen with frustration.

Hah shut his eyes tight and tried to block out the whole ugly situation.

Hid, instead, tried to analyze what had happened. "Why did they do this to me?" he asked. "How will I pay my bills?"

Finally, Hah reopened his eyes. What was wrong with this picture? "Where are Snivel and Scurvy? Do they know something we don't know?"

Hid scoffed. "They're just rats. What would they know that we don't know? We're people. We're smarter than they are. We have all the answers. They're just rats."

"Precisely," Hah answered. "They're rats, and as such, should know instinctively just what The Boss and his lackey, The Accountant Andersen, are thinking. They have a distinct advantage over us in understanding just what is going on."

"Maybe you're right," said Hid. "Let's look for them."

So they set out into the maze in search of the rats.

While Hid and Hah were walking through the maze, Snivel and Scurvy had already come upon new cheese. Sometimes it takes a rat to smell a rat. They instinctively understood The Boss's next move, and in a short time had found their way to the cheese.

In the meantime, back in the maze, Hid and Hah were assigning blame to each other in losing the supply of cheese. They couldn't see that The Boss was responsible because they were still deluded in the belief that they were all working toward a common goal. That the success of the corporation would ensure their personal gain.

Sometimes Hid and Hah would imagine Snivel and Scurvy finding the cheese and taking all the credit. The rats were not team players. Maybe they should adopt the same policy of self-aggrandizement. Every man for himself, as it were.

Hid grew tired walking through the maze. He wanted to go back to his cubicle, which was familiar and comfortable. The maze could be dangerous.

Hid convinced Hah to go back to the cubicles with him. Maybe the cheese had returned. Maybe it was just a test to gauge their level of tolerance.

Hah had a fear of failure, so he agreed to return to their old familiar cubicles with Hid. Maybe the cheese would be back tomorrow.

So, every day the two loyal employees returned to their cubicles to devote themselves to the futile quest for cheese.

Every day they searched in the same places and came up empty-handed. They went home frustrated, and fought with their wives.

They tried to deny what had happened to them, but it was no use. They were losing sleep every night, and they were cranky at work.

They had nightmares about how they would pay their bills. It would only be a matter of time before they might lose their jobs altogether.

But Hid and Hah loyally reported to their office every day. Even if they had nothing to do. Even if they were just moving papers around on their desks. Even if they were surfing the Web to find jokes to cheer themselves up and e-mail to their fellow employees, who were suffering from the same sense of frustration.

Hid said, "Maybe we're not trying hard enough. I know that the cheese is here, somewhere."

So the next day, he brought a sledgehammer to work and demolished his cubicle, looking for cheese behind the walls and under the floor.

Hah, who wanted to call the company nurse to intervene in Hid's lunacy, instead chose to ignore the fit of madness. He had worked himself into an inertia that bordered on catatonia. So each day he sat at his desk and stared into the photo of the rainbow. Day by day, he grew increasingly more depressed.

By now, the loyal employees were weak with hunger and paralyzed with fear.

Hah had to do something. He said, "Hid, look at us. We're pathetic. They've changed the rules and we were unable to cope. We've become inert. We have to change, or die. Which will it be?"

Hid was jolted by this dose of reality. "You're right," he answered. "But I'm afraid. I'll just stay here and wait for the cheese to come back."

"I know how you feel, but I have to force myself to go back into the maze. Maybe there's more cheese out there." So Hah reluctantly climbed back into his business suit and running shoes, and he walked back into the maze.

Hah motivated himself by visualizing a supply of new cheese. He thought of all the time he had wasted in the office wallowing in depression and said, "Don't get mad. Get even."

Hah was walking into the maze cautiously. He wasn't fully convinced that the cheese wouldn't return to the cubicle on its own. Maybe he hadn't given it enough time.

Hah understood his colleague's reluctance to return to the maze. It was scary and unfamiliar. He picked up a rock and used it to scratch another of The Boss's mottoes on the wall of the maze. It read:

If You Do Not Steal,
You Only Have As Much Cheese As
The Rats And Loyal Employees.

He began to feel empowered again, just a little. And he continued to forge into the maze, into the unknown.

The Boss was looking down at his loyal employee as Hah set out on his journey through the maze. Hah was beginning to show some initiative. He might be just the kind of employee who could be groomed for an upper management position. The Boss had his eye on him. He would motivate him to find more cheese, as a test of his ability. He spoke to Hah from above the maze, and Hah looked up at The Boss in disbelief.

"Enjoy the process and fulfillment will be your reward," The Boss said to Hah.

Hah looked up at the mythical figure of The Boss looming over him. Recognizing him. Offering sage advice.

"But what about the cheese?" Hah asked.

"That's mine," The Boss answered. "I'm The Boss."

"But what about us? What is our reward?" asked the loyal employee.

"You were meant for other things. Like hard work. Continue in the maze. The work will make you free," said The Boss.

The Boss reached down and, with a great hand, scrawled a message on the wall for Hah. It read:

You Can't Steal The Cheese
If You Do Not Make
The Rats And Small Men Fear You.

Hah looked at the wall and thought about it.

He couldn't follow that rule just yet. He had been brainwashed into thinking ethical thoughts, and he would have to abandon all conscience and reason to play the game by The Boss's rules. He wasn't yet ready to assume a management role.

As Hah continued through the maze, he found scraps of cheese here and there. Not enough to pile up and bring in for processing. But just enough to sustain him in this quest. He noticed, however, that this cheese was different from the cheese he had eaten in the cubicle. This cheese tasted good.

The Boss was looking down on his loyal employee, and reached out to write a new rule on the wall of the maze. It said:

Smell The Cheese Often So You're Only Stealing The New Cheese.

Finally, a rule from The Boss that made sense. This was a motto that he could follow.

Hah continued through the maze. He found no sign of Snivel and Scurvy, but he was finding lots of small pieces of new cheese along the way. It was not enough cheese to collect for processing, but it was enough to feed and revive him. He was finally feeling better and able to think more clearly. It was only a matter of time before he would locate a supply of cheese. He was certain that he had turned the corner.

The Boss grew pleased with his progress and again he reached down to inscribe a new rule on the wall. It read:

Keep The Workers Moving So They
Find You More New Cheese.

Hah looked down the long road ahead. What if there was no new cheese? How could he keep his job? What would become of him down this unfamiliar path? And what about all the progress he had made? Maybe The Boss didn't see him as management material. How would he ever become a big cheese now?

Hah felt a fear of the unknown. A fear of losing his employment. A fear of mounting unpaid bills. He would have to find more cheese.

As if on schedule, a large arm extended over his head to write on the wall before him:

Make The Workers Fear You
So They Feel Entrapped.

The Boss was right. Fear is a powerful motivator, and he continued walking through the maze, looking for cheese.

Hah knew there was more cheese in the maze, somewhere. The rats had probably found it by now. He thought of the rats, sitting fat and full on a mountain of cheese.

As if reading his mind, The Boss reached out and wrote a new rule on the wall. It was:

Imagining Myself Enjoying
All The New Cheese
Keeps Me On Top Of The Game.

The loyal employee began to shudder. Big Brother was watching him, and he wasn't delivering the goods. It was only a matter of time before The Boss pulled the plug and he was left unemployed.

The Boss noticed Hah's slight change in demeanor. The truth was The Boss needed *them* as much as they needed him. Maybe even more. But The Boss couldn't let them know that. He wrote:

Let Them Eat Old Cheese.
The New Cheese Is All Mine.

Hah began to think about Hid. He wondered if his colleague had found any more cheese, or if he was getting enough to eat. Hah felt it was time to return to the cubicle, just to check on him. He picked up some small bits of cheese along the way, and stuffed them into his pockets for Hid. Then he retraced his steps and walked back to the cubicle.

Hid was sitting alone at his desk, looking hungry and thin. Hah offered Hid the bits of new cheese, but Hid refused.

"I don't think I'd like the new cheese. I'm happy eating the crumbs of the old cheese that I find in my desk. I'm not going to adjust to a whole new way of doing things. I'm just going to tough the situation out until the old ways return," said Hid.

Hah felt sadness for his colleague. Hid could be stubborn and resistant to change. He tried to convince Hid to leave the cubicle, to follow him to the maze. But Hid was adamant about waiting in the office for the cheese to return. Hah didn't want to be passive like Hid, caught in a stagnant routine, so he decided to return to the maze alone.

The Boss was pleased with Hah's demonstration of self-motivation. It was further proof that he was management material and could be groomed to assume a leadership role within the system. The Boss wanted to let Hah know that he was doing the right thing by returning to the maze, so he reached out and wrote:

Keep Them Trapped In The Maze
Eating Old Cheese
While I Savor The New Cheese.

Hah was beginning to grow a bit more comfortable with The Boss and his new rules. While he had been happy working in his cubicle, eating old cheese, it was only when he was forced out into the maze that he realized that the cheese he had been happily eating had grown stale.

Being out in the maze, finding scraps of new cheese had taught him there was more to life than just old cheese.

He had developed a taste for new cheese, just like that connoisseur, The Boss.

Hah, therefore, began to grow resentful when he read The Boss's new rule:

Feed Workers Old Cheese
So That They Can Find You
The New Cheese.

That philosophy might still work with Hid, who was cowering in his old cubicle.

But Hah was now a man of the world, traveling through the maze alone. Savoring the experience. Tasting and enjoying bits of new cheese.

He was beginning to feel entrepreneurial, looking out for his own interests. Maybe he wasn't just a worker after all. Maybe he had management potential. He hoped that The Boss was watching him now.

There was lots of new cheese to taste in the maze. He only had to persevere to find it.

Hah hadn't found new cheese yet, but he was encouraged by his quest. It would only be a matter of time before he found a new supply of cheese.

Hah smiled to himself. Walking through the maze in search of new cheese had invigorated him. Built his confidence. He felt certain that new cheese was just around the bend in the maze.

The Boss smiled, too. Hah was adapting to change. Learning new lessons. Remaining faithful and useful to the corporate cause. It was only a matter of time before he could be entrusted with the mantle of management. Hah could be a useful executive to help in The Boss's ultimate plan. He reached out and wrote a new message on the wall:

Tease The Workers
With A Taste Of New Cheese
To Keep Them On Course.

Hah walked a little faster. He had wasted too much precious time hiding in his cubicle, waiting for the cheese to reappear. He stopped to pick up and eat the chunks of new cheese that The Boss cleverly dropped in his path to keep him motivated.

Hah would soon come upon a new cache of cheese. New cheese. And *he* would earn the respect of The Boss by bringing it in for processing.

He could hardly suspect that The Boss anticipated his every move. That The Boss was planning his next move for him, guiding him through the maze by subliminal direction. The Boss would soon put him in position to deliver the biggest load of cheese so far. So much cheese that The Boss would never want for cheese again.

Hah turned the corner of the maze to behold a mountain of cheese just waiting for him to carve it out, chunk by chunk, and carry it back to the processing center.

Hah was certain that his fortune was made. Surely he would be promoted to "Big Cheese" now! He finally felt like an integral member of the team. Then he saw his old associates, Snivel and Scurvy, cutting chunks of cheese. He then knew that he had finally found his goal. His cheese.

Hah would have to return to the cubicle to get Hid. There was far too much cheese for him to process alone, and he would need Hid to lift and carry the load back to the processing center.

Hah finally understood just how The Boss must feel. He, too, was a Boss, but on a smaller scale. He was moving up the ladder toward success.

The rules had changed. And he had changed with them. He saw the writing on the wall and it was:

THE WRITING ON THE WALL

Greed Happens
I Keep Stealing The Cheese

Ignore My Greed
Keep Piling Up Cheese

Monitor The Workers
Smell The Cheese Often So I'm Sure I'm
Getting All The New Cheese

Keep Changing The Rules
Feed Your Workers Old Cheese And Enjoy All
The New Cheese Yourself

Control The Maze
Steal The New Cheese

Enjoy Control
Savor The Game And Enjoy All The New Cheese

Be Ready To Control The Game
Keep Stealing The Cheese

The Boss smiled. Only *he* knew that he had manipulated the situation and called all the shots.

For now, the rats, Hah, and under his direction, Hid too, would diligently cut the cheese into bite-size pieces and carry them to the processing center.

Only The Boss knew what would happen next. That with the help of his lackey, The Accountant Andersen, The Boss would steal all the cheese, every last bit of it. That The Accountant Andersen would move all of the cheese offshore to unmarked accounts.

Only then would The Boss hang his head in shame and declare that the company was bankrupt. Kaput!

It had worked before. And it would work again.

And with that, The Boss wrote his final declaration upon the wall:

Keep Stealing The Cheese
And Enjoy It!

The Boss picked up his briefcase and climbed into the corporate jet. As he entered the cabin, he looked back out the door at Accountant Andersen and called out his final words of wisdom:

"Shred the evidence!"

When the smoke finally cleared, Hid, Hah, and Snivel and Scurvy were left with nothing. No job. No company. No pension. No cheese.

The Boss and The Accountant Andersen were eventually indicted under the revised penalties for white-collar crime and were sentenced to serve twenty years at a minimum security prison.

Hid, Hah, and Snivel and Scurvy bumped into each other on line at the unemployment office, while waiting to receive their weekly cheese rations.

"How are you doing? Any bites on a new job?" Hid asked Hah.

"No. So many companies have closed. Gone bankrupt. All the bosses are in prison," said Hah.

"That's good. They got what they deserved," Hid said with a wistful smile.

Snivel and Scurvy said nothing. They never did. They were just rats.

"But where does that leave us? I don't know what to do. I can't find a job, my savings are running out, and my 401K is worthless," said Hid sadly. "Do you have any ideas?"

Hah, who had become more like The Boss in the final days of the company scandal, had been spending his time on the unemployment line devising new ideas to solve his financial problems. His stock options had become worthless with the demise of the company, and his savings were rapidly diminishing. He had lost his faith in the corporate system, and he had no trust in the stock market nor cheese to invest there. Where would he find his cheese?

Where had he gone wrong? How had he lost his cheese and his savings? And why was The Boss so rich? How had The Boss made his fortune? Hah pondered that point endlessly. Hah had admired The Boss and his creative methods of problem solving. He had to laugh at himself for being so gullible as to believe The Boss's lies.

Hah thought that he was building toward the future. He had been doing everything right. Being a member of the team. Working long hours. Getting the job done. How could he have been so stupid?

The Boss had probably socked away enough cheese to last a lifetime. And the workers were left holding the bag, with nothing to show for their long years of hard work.

Hah thought about The Boss. How had he found his cheese? Hah recognized that The Boss had devised a corporate scheme. This was now impossible, given the changing business laws. But The Boss had also developed a set of rules. Maybe the answers could be found here.

Hah would have to develop his own set of rules, ones he could use in the new business climate. But where to begin?

Hah recognized that he could no longer trust the system to provide support. He had to trust in his own ability to solve his own problems. And that presented the first rule:

Believe In Yourself

Hah began to see the wisdom in this plan, and had faith in his own convictions. He thought hard and composed the next rule:

Don't Let Anyone Change You

Even though he had lost his job and was struggling to maintain his lifestyle, he recognized that he could not let these reverses shake his beliefs. He couldn't let his troubles (or challenges) defeat him. And that suggested the next rule:

Never Give Up

Hah realized that he had to remain strong to turn the tide. He had to remain constantly alert to recognize the opportunities. He could not hide away in his house, waiting for things to happen. Which could be stated as:

You Have To Stay In The Game

You have to be in it to win it. As long as you're out there, trying, you increase your chances of success, which Hah could also phrase as:

You Have To Keep A Lot Of Balls Up In The Air.
The More You Have, The More Chances You Have To Catch Them

But Hah realized ideas aren't everything. His years in the corporation had taught him that success was dependent upon hard work, which he described as:

Success Is 10% Inspiration and 90% Perspiration

Hah began to understand that the only way to succeed was to take responsibility for his own actions. Become entrepreneurial. He could no longer put his trust in The Boss or the system. He had to have strength of character to turn away from all that was familiar and forge a new path to success. This could be summed up in his final rule, which was:

A Smart Man Knows
When To Stop Being Stupid

Finally Hah had found some rules to believe in. Because they were his. He scribbled his rules down on a scrap of paper, and then stuffed it into his pocket.

Hah turned to his former colleague, Hid, and was now prepared to pass his wisdom along to him.

"I have a few ideas about how to succeed in business today. I'm going to write a book, and put it all down. There are seven simple rules that anyone can follow. Even you. But you'll have to wait until it is published before I can sell you one. Because," declared Hah...

"I don't share *my* ideas
with anyone."

the end...
or a fresh start?

A Dissection
Recreational Break

When Martha finished writing the story down, painstakingly editing it for content and accuracy (after all, it had to be perfect), she collated copies, bound them in covers cleverly crafted from discarded license plates, and distributed them (packed in baskets with freshly baked chocolate chip cookies) to the members of the club during the afternoon recreational break. Not bad for a morning's work.

The group sat together in a corner of the court-yard, leaning against the heavy metal fence, and examined the books. It took them only a short time to read the entire thing. No editing was required, as Martha was also an expert proofreader.

"Bernie, what do you think of your idea?" Martha asked coyly.

"It's perfect," he said.

"Of course it is," Martha smiled back. "Especially the cheesy feel-good ending. They'll think they're getting useful advice. They'll buy more books! And we'll look good to the parole board. It's a win/win situation."

Martha passed out metal mugs of iced chamomile tea adorned with sprigs of fresh mint that she had grown herself in a corner of the basketball court (and had cleverly disguised as weeds).

The group began to kid each other about being members of the most exclusive club in the world.

"If you're indicted, you're invited," Ken Lie said with a laugh.

"So, who were you in the story? Snivel, Scurvy, Hid or Hah?" asked Jack Grubby.

"We're all The Boss!" said Bernie Embers. "That's why we wrote the book."

"But there are elements of all of the characters in each of us," said Martha. "At times I feel like Snivel, because I should have smelled a rat. That awful Peter Backtothewall and his assistant, Douglas Fanfare, turned state's evidence and let me take the rap, just to save their cushy hides. I think they were just looking for a way to get their names into all the columns. Be careful what you wish for, I always say....

"So now we're all in here together. The media can't get enough of this story. People are just eating it up. And just wait until our book comes out. The press will have a field day. But as long as they get the title of the book right and spell my name correctly, I don't care. We'll have the last laugh," she said gleefully.

"Sometimes I've acted like Scurvy," John Rigs joined in. "Blindly running ahead. I remember feeling that way during my 'perp walk.' I didn't want to make eye contact with anyone I knew, so I just ran toward the courthouse."

"I know what you mean," said Sam Weasel. "I felt the same way on my way into the indictment hearing. At a time like that I wish I had been Hid, and had stayed safely in my office. But it's too late for regrets. We just have to get through this time here. It's good that we're all in here together. I don't know what I would do without you guys," he said with a catch in his throat.

"I remember when I had a rough time with change," said Dennis Kozlousy. "It was during the investigation. I had just been named to the board of the Whitney Museum, and they had the nerve to blow that little matter about my art collection and unpaid taxes out of proportion. You know what Leona said about that, 'Only the little people pay taxes.' Do you suppose that she was referring to Hid and Hah?" Dennis smiled. "I guess I can laugh about it now, because it doesn't pay to cry."

"'Looking for new cheese' can be another term for an unexpected change of employment. That's a nice way to describe what all of us are doing in here. We used to be CEOs. Now we're the authors of motivational literature," said Gary Whining.

"Hid reminds me of a friend of mine. His company was in shambles, but he refused to see it until they pulled the plug," John remembered.

"Are you talking about me again?" asked Ken.

"No. I think he means me this time," Joe Buriedinero replied.

"Heck, it could be any of us," said Bernie. "I have an old saying. 'You can't cry over spilled millions!' Or billions, for that matter. At the end of the day, it all comes down to a bunch of zeros."

Some of the club members who had been quiet at the beginning now felt comfortable enough to speak up. After all, if they looked at Bernie's losses, their own felt insignificant by comparison.

"I feel like I should have been more like Snivel," Alfred Tubman sighed. "If I had, I would have sniffed out what Deedee was up to. She seemed so refined when all along she was ruthless. I'm in here while she's strolling Madison Avenue in an ankle bracelet. I just hope she doesn't run into Judy in Hermès! She'll tear her eyes out."

"I know I'm in here by mistake. I didn't do anything wrong. I didn't lose anyone's life savings. I just gave them harmless stock advice. How could I know that the stocks would tank?" Jack complained.

"Because you were at all the board meetings, silly," said Ken.

"That's right," said Bernie. "We're all in this together."

"I wish my family had known about the cheese story," John interjected. "We didn't want to see the changes coming, and we were caught with our pants down. If I knew then what I know now, I would have done things differently. Been less conspicuous. Joined a country club instead of building my own golf course."

"I can see now that most of us had elements of Hid in us. We didn't change and remained in the same place for too long. If we had been more like Scurvy, we could have moved quickly onto new things, and stayed one step ahead of the SEC," said Andy Fastbuck.

"Change is happening everywhere, and we need to learn to adjust to it so that we can succeed once more," said Jeff Skimming.

"I know it sounds subversive," Michael Kopout confessed, "but sometimes I wish that I had been more like Hid, and remained safely ensconced in my office, quietly doing my job. If I had done that, I would have never found myself in this place today."

"That's not true. You *did* hole up within your office, doing your job, and minting your bogus partnerships," said Andy. "It was only when the Feds put on the heat and took away your little nest egg that you crumbled and copped a plea. That's how you took us down with you, and now we're all in here together. We should be resentful over that, but with Bernie's help, we've seen the light and found it within our hearts to forgive you. But we're still happy that you had to give your money back!"

"I *still* don't know why I'm here," Jeff said, sadly. "I didn't do anything wrong. The wheels were already in motion when I took over for Ken. I only led the firm for a few months. I should never have been the one to take all the blame. Ken, I think it was all your fault."

"Jeff, I don't know why you want to lay the blame on me. I was an excellent CEO. The business was growing and thriving under my leadership. Didn't you get rich working there? Didn't Andy? And even people as low in the pecking order as Michael got a brief chance to taste the millions. It's not my fault that things began to go bad," said Ken.

"I feel the same way," said Sam. "I didn't do anything illegal. I was only protecting my family. Cloneim was mine to do with as I pleased. I built it, made it. I could sell my stock whenever I wanted, and I could advise my family members to do the same."

"I agree," Martha chimed in. "And the same privilege should be extended to close friends. When you were dating my daughter, I always hoped it would work out. I would have liked you as my son-in-law. And besides, I always thought of you as family, so it would have been nice if you *had* called me about the stock. As it is, they didn't believe me, so we're all in here together, anyway." Martha's expression grew resigned. "But let's not get mired up in self-pity. I find that hard work, and lots of it, can distract me from the emptiness in my life. Let's talk about the book."

"I think we have applied the lessons of the cheese story. We're finding new ways to achieve success within our new environment. Just look at our fledgling publishing career. Who ever could have imagined that we would be in the publishing business from in here?" said Bernie proudly.

"I would. I've been in the publishing business everywhere. I'm always in charge. That's why I called it 'Omnipotent,'" said Martha.

"What do you see as our next career move?" Jack asked.

"We should go into multifaceted marketing," Martha began. "We can develop an adorable line of tin hostessware," she said examining the metal mug more closely.

"I can see this as a tabletop collection of dishes, beakers, bowls and mugs, with some clever serving pieces and flatware. They can be easily manufactured in the license plate workshop. Next, we branch into coordinating napkins and tablecloths, cut from the uniform fabric. Stripes are very big this season.

"Then we develop a corresponding group of bed linens, with matching pajamas. We'll base them upon the design of our prison uniforms and bedding. It will be easier for the inmates to make them in the sweatshop if they're sewing familiar garments. We'll just double up production with the uniforms and sheets, and apply the savings to our profits. And later we move into a grouping of upholstered furniture. It can all be manufactured on the inside.

"We'll pay our fellow inmates in cigarettes, or my famous home-baked cookies. Whichever they prefer. They'd certainly choose that over the 11 cents they'd be making if they were cranking out license plates for the state.

"We can market our products at Not OKmart as the 'Martha Stewed Jailhouse Style Collection,' if they don't go into liquidation before we ship the first line.

"And that's just the start. I have a million other ideas for ways to make money while we're in here. We'll develop a lifestyle magazine, and syndicate a TV show. Or several.

"I can see a cooking show as being most beneficial to us all. It would certainly elevate the level of cuisine that they serve in the dining room, or cafeteria, as they call it. I keep forgetting their quaint names for everything here.

"You'll only have to pay me my standard licensing fee for the use of my name and designs. But you can have your families wire the money directly from your off-shore accounts into mine," she said with a smile.

"But getting back to our first venture," Dennis interrupted. "The book. We have to market it correctly. What would you recommend?"

"I think I have the answer," said Bernie, taking over the floor. "The key is in the numbers. We have to sell it in large quantities, especially to groups.

"We can start right here. Let's approach the warden about holding 'cheese' seminars and discussion groups for the inmates. We can make the meetings festive, serve wine and cheese. We'll call the discussion sessions 'Whine and Cheese Parties.' The correctional system will have to buy lots of the books to distribute to the inmates. If we can institute a program throughout the penal system, on a national basis, we'll sell a ton of books.

"From there we approach the government. Ken, you know the Bushes. And you're solid with the Democrats, too. They can be your account. Politicians can use this motivational tool. And it's ideal for the bureaucracy. It will keep them in line. Our program should be marketed as a lifesaver. It can prevent the members of the Postal Service from 'going postal'!

"I'm sure we all still have friends at the heads of corporations. That sale is a natural. And we can hire our fellow inmates to do the telemarketing. Then Martha can plug it on her TV shows. Just give it time. This thing can be big. Maybe even bigger than our last business ventures...."

"Bernie's right," Martha agreed. "They may have beat the crepe out of us, but we'll rise like a soufflé and win again!"

the end, for now

Share It With Everyone

We hope that you have enjoyed this book and have learned something valuable from its lessons. We know that we have.

If you have reacted to this book in any way (positively, negatively, or with revulsion) we would like you to know that all profits from the book are being donated to a worthy cause, The Allenwood 13 Defense Fund. This non-profit slush fund, we mean charity, will pay for the legal defense of 13 former corporate leaders who have been wrongfully convicted of white-collar crimes. We were only doing our jobs.

Please recommend this book to all your friends so that we can pay our lawyers, as we cannot afford to mount a competent defense with our own funds. We don't share *our* money with anyone.

About the Author

Ilene Hochberg, B.S., B.S.A.*, is an internationally bestselling author whose parody books help millions of people laugh over the absurdities of life, and enjoy healthier times with more success and less stress. They say that laughter is the best medicine....

Her examination of the anthropomorphism of animals (i.e. treating our pets as people) has been met with great acclaim. Her books *Dogue, Catmopolitan, Vanity Fur, Forbabes,* and *Good Mousekeeping* are perennial favorites.

Her education includes a B.S. in Design and Environmental Analysis from Cornell University. In a remarkable case of only *two* degrees of separation, Ms. Hochberg served as a guest speaker for Cornell's Entrepreneur of the Year Program, a forum designed to encourage entrepreneurial ventures, with Kenneth Blanchard, Ph.D. Dr. Blanchard was co-author of the bestselling book series, *The One Minute Manager* with Spencer Johnson, M.D., who was the author of the original bestseller, *Who Moved My Cheese?*

Her books have been featured in the media including CNN, *Good Morning America, Newsweek, Forbes, The Wall Street Journal, Vanity Fair, Good Housekeeping, Cosmopolitan, Architectural Digest, Advertising Age, The New York Times Bestseller List, Publishers Weekly, Regis and Kathie Lee, Donahue, Jeopardy, Hollywood Squares, Designing Women* and *Good Morning* Everywhere....

Ms. Hochberg is a member of Mensa, has been an instructor at the Parsons School of Design, holds a Black Belt in shopping, and is a confirmed knitter. In other words, she is the ideal person to have written this book.

*B.S.A. stands for Bull**** Artist.